Lit From Within

Carol Beth Thompson

BookLeaf Publishing

India | USA | UK

Presentation by *BookLeaf Publishing*

Web: www.bookleafpub.com

E-mail: info@bookleafpub.com

ISBN: 9789360949280

First edition 2024

Dad, you were right -

*"One poem, on one page, in one book is a
great start, but you are more than one
page... you are the whole damn book! So
go. Write your life. Just make sure you
always right yourself happy..."*

ACKNOWLEDGEMENT

Thank you -

To everyone who encouraged me to keep going when I didn't think I could.

For believing in me, when I was having trouble believing in myself.

For helping me out of the dark & for sticking around after I pushed you away.

And for reminding me to breathe a lot more, smile more, laugh (A LOT) more & love more often.

PREFACE

Life is short...
So I quit asking myself "Why?" so much --
And started asking myself "Why not!?"

• A LIFE BEAT •

S haring

M usic

I nspires

L ife's

E nergy!

SO.... SMILE!

• HA HA • HA HA •

- • L earn

- • A ccept

- • U nderstand

- • G row

- • H eal

- • T each

- • E mpower

- • R ise

Laughter can Heal -
  the Mind,
    the Heart,
      the Body
        & the Soul.

• HEAVEN and HELL •

She only wanted to love you,
  Yet you pushed her away.
She offered her time to listen to you,
  But you had nothing real to say.
She offered you her hand,
  To help you up off the ground.
While she was lifting you up,
  You were just pulling her down.
The times you were lost and lonely,
  And you could see no end in sight,
She reached out & took your hand
  While she offered you her light.
She offered you her back,
  To help carry some of the weight.
She realized it was crushing her,
  But by then it was just too late.
And now you're not weighed down,
  Now things are going so well -
She showed you there is a heaven,
  And you just left her there in hell.

• WOLVES and SHEEP •

- F ake as fuck

- R otten souled

- I gnorant liars

•E ndlessly plotting

- N everending excuses

- D ope fiending

•S cumbags

• GOOD TWIST • BAD WORD •

- **N** ice

- **I** ntelligent

- **G** irl (or Guy)

- **G** etting

- **E** verything

- **R** ight

Yes I am,
everyday!

• WANTS •

I want you -
 I want you for
 your smile,
  your eyes,
   your voice,
    your laugh.
 I want you for
      your heart,
       your warmth,
        your kindness,
         your compassion.
 I want you when
        you're happy,
        you're sad,
         you're failing,
          you're succeeding.
  I want you for
        your flaws,
         your visions,
          your realness,
           your selflessness.
  I want you for
         You.

• NOT LIKE ME •

You will never
find another like me -
ever!
And you know it.
Nobody will ever come
close to matching
the amount of
Love, Loyalty, Respect,
Trust, Work, Time,
Faith, Honesty & Friendship
that I can give.
Nobody.
There's only ONE place
where ALL of that
can be found...
And thats right here.

• I AM •

Some say that I am strong
  Others say I am weak
Some say I am blunt with the truth
  Others say I am a liar
Some say I am full of confidence
  Others say that I'm full of doubt
Some say I am loud & obnoxious
  Others say I am quiet & reserved
Some say I am fun to be around
  Others say that I'm a drag
Some say that can I kick ass
  Others say I get my ass kicked
Some say that I'm light & up beat
  Others say I'm dark & a downer
Some say I'm looking happier
  Others say that I'm looking sad
I say that they are all correct -
    I am.

• SOMETIMES • EVERYTIME •

<pre>
                Sometimes
                   I
                  Cry
                 When
                   I
                 Think
                About
                 My
                Dad,
               But
             Everytime
            I
          Smile
</pre>

          I miss you Dad.

• DON'T MIND •

Hi...

If you don't mind

Don't mind me

'Cause I don't mind me

And I won't mind you neither

• HEART and BRAIN •

BRAIN:

Hey, Heart... How do you know this is "the one"?
That this time its for real?
How do you know that this isn't just another shitty deal?
Weren't they all "the one" in the beginning?...
Heart..?

HEART: . . . .

And she hasn't spoke a word since

• TRASH •

Hello.
  My name is Trash.
Looking back that's all I see.
   Kept around until needed,
Then used and discarded -
   Like Trash.
Few are nice enough to put me in a bin.
   Others throw me down wherever
   they're at -
Either way I'm tossed aside just the same...
   Hello...
My name is Trash.

• SLAP THIS BITCH •

If you see me and I'm with him -
   Slap This Bitch.
Remind me how fucking grim
My life was when I was with him.
I'd be a fool to go do this again -
   So, please Slap This Bitch

If I'm asking if he's been around -
   Come Slap This Bitch.
Ask how many times we've gone rounds,
With me always picking myself up off the
ground.
Ask what what made me stick around -
   Then, please, Slap This Bitch.

If you hear me still speaking his name -
   Help me and Slap This Bitch.
Tell me that he's only playing games,
And that going back would just be shame.
And I'd have no one but myself to blame -
   So,please, Slap This Bitch.

• I FEEL LIKE •

•a Fool • an Ass • an Idiot • a Jerk•
a Moron • a Sucker • a Twit • a Boneyard • a
Clown • a Dim Wit •
 a Dolt • a Dope • a Dunce • a Bird
Brain • a Blockhead • a Clod • an
Ignoramus • an Imbecile • a Sap •
a Nincompoop • a Numb Skull • a
Schelp • a Simpleton • a Half Wit •
a Lame Brain • a Jackass • a Bozo
• a Dweeb • a Schmuck • a Dummy
• a Dumbass • a Nimrod • a Schaub
• a Putz • I'm Stupid & I'm Dumb... whenever
I'm with you.

• TESTERS •

Some people are here in life to test
every aspect about us.
To see if we will break or bend.
To test the limits of
our Character, our Temper,
our Loyalty, our Pride, our Honesty,
our Faith, our Honor, our Strengths,
our Weaknesses & our Self Worth.
They'll test us
Physically, Emotionally, Mentally,
Spiritually, Financially & Materially.
They push us to the edge,
To find out if we push back
Or get pushed over.
Yet, while they were learning
all about us,
We're learning & remembering
things about ourselves as well.
We learn that our
Loyalty, Honesty, Pride,
Character, Faith & Honor
are Unshakable.
We are reminded that
Only we can control our
Temper, our Reactions &

How we Feel & See ourselves.
We learned that our Strengths,
Just get stronger,
And our Weaknesses
Are just stepping stones
to new Strengths
We learn that
Physical, Spiritual, Emotional
& Mental Pain can be healed.
And we're reminded that
Financial & Material things
are Replaceable.
And yet, the last test,
Is one that we give to ourselves,
But fail repeatedly.
Because to pass,
We need to Let Go, Walk Away &
apply what we've learned
towards our future.
But, usually -
We get stuck in the past,
Failing our future selves
& learning those harsh tests of life
For nothing...

• TALKING and JUMPING •

Whatever words that I speak to you should stop
right there.
   The words I say should never be
   spoken from your mouth to
   someone else's ears -
Not even God's.
   Its not yours to speak on or about
   with anyone but me,
Because it's MY business you're speaking about.
   On the other side of that equation,
To the one who hears I'm speaking about them -
   Before you get your feelers hurt
   by what someone says I said,
Even if you heard it from God's mouth -
   Why aren't you talking to me
   about it first?
At least come check and see if I even said it!
   And if I did, did they even quote
   me right?
Instead you take take jump to conclusions
   And get your feelers all twisted
   and hurt.
So you can go ahead and keep talking ABOUT
me,
   Because you won't be talking to

me anymore.
And you can keep on jumping to conclusions
about me,
  Because I no longer care what
  your feelers are hurt for.
So keep on talking and keep
on jumping, folks.

• TO ALL THOSE BEFORE

•

To all the beers I've ever chugged before,
To all the empties strewn across my apartment
floor -
  We'd pick 'em up & cash 'em in,
  So we could do it all again -
To go get more beers down at the corner store.

To all the ho's I have had to put in check before,
Why the hell do you look so fucking surprised
for?
  I told you to shut your fucking lips,
  But you kept on talking stupid shit.
And so I pushed your ass right out the door.

To all those pills I've popped before,
To the ones from inside the bathroom drawer -
  Supposed to put me in a "better"
  space,
  But I can't even feel my face -
To crawl, puke & pass out on the kitchen floor.

To all the Weed I've rolled before,
Wrapped up nicely in a joint, blunt or cone -
  Weed always lightens up my mood,

I need to get some drinks & food -
To get rid of the cotton mouth I've got going on.

• HAPPY IS POSSIBLE •

- F inally

- R ealizing

- I n

- Every

- N ew

- D ay

- S taying

- H appy

- I s

- P ossible

• DROWNING •

Whether you're drowning in water,

Or drowning in emotions,

They both can leave you -

Breathless and fighting for air,

Reaching out for something,

Touching nothing's all you ever do.

Turned around and upside down

And -

In the end,

Both can kill you.

• WE ARE HOMELESSNESS •

H usbands & Wives
O utcasted Soldiers
M others & Fathers
E lderly & Young
L ost Souls
E x Convicts
S avage Strangers
S inners & Saints
N urses & Care Givers
E xiled Educators
S tep "others"
S urviving Siblings

• COLD SHOULDERS •

All she wanted was to be there for you
To help with the struggles you were going
through
She offered her back to help carry the weight
And her shoulder to lean on if the tears should
escape
Her ear to listen anytime, any day
To hear the words you have to say
And to help you through the dark & cold
She gave you her hand for you to hold
And no matter what you might've been going
through
She never once judged or looked down on you
She only offered help because she cared
And your sudden cold shoulder caught her
unprepared
It seemed as though you had nothing more to say
With weight still on her back, you just walked
away
While on her shoulder, the tears you cried still
shown
As you left her there confused, in the dark, all
alone
When you see her again some day

You'll see what happened when you walked
away
Once, a warm light shone in her eyes, like a
flame
But now something about her just isn't the same
From her you got love & from you she got a
cold shoulder
Which made the fire in her eyes a bit darker & a
bit colder

www.ingramcontent.com/pod-product-compliance
Lightning Source LLC
Chambersburg PA
CBHW071242140726
47996CB00007B/2719